Wizards

Book One

The Awakening Tales

Paula Matthew CSJ

MW00813984

The Indigo Wizard

The Awakening Tales

Paula Matthew CSJ

Tales of the Indigo Wizard: The Awakening Tales

Copyright © 2010 by Anamchara Books a Division of Harding House Publishing Service, Inc. All rights reserved. No part of this publication may be reproduced or transmitted in any form or by any means, electronic or mechanical, including photocopying, recording, taping, or any information storage and retrieval system, without permission from the publisher.

Anamchara Books
220 Front Street
Vestal, NY 13850

First Printing

9 8 7 6 5 4 3 2 1

ISBN: 978-1-933630-77-9

Author: Paula Matthew CSJ.
Interior and cover design by MK Bassett-Harvey.
Illustrations by Keith Rosko and MK Bassett-Harvey.

To the Reader

These stories were written for you by Golden Quill,
scribe to the Indigo Wizard.
This volume contains one year of tales,
twelve months of the Wizard's wisdom.

Turn the page—
start your journey.

Take the scribe's blessing,
from quill to heart,
and may you grow
in wisdom.

Contents

Tale one

The I Manifesting Itself

The Glen was alive with expectation. The birds held their breath, and Fawn stood frozen, staring at something tiny and green hanging from a twig. The bees hovered over the branch, humming their welcome.

"Almost time!" Owl said. "Get ready!"

Fox, Snake, Frog, Rabbit, Grasshopper, and Bear joined the others, their attention all focused on that one small, green point, a gold-zippered chrysalis. It trembled on its branch. . . .

Pop!

The delicate green skin split and something tawny-orange emerged.

Stretch!

The crumpled orange velvet unfurled into two great wings.

"Ohhh." The animals let out their breath. "A new creation has come to the Glen," they whispered to each other.

The newest member of their community looked around, startled by the circle of faces staring up at her. "Where am I?" She peered over her shoulder at the wide flutter of wings. "*Who* am I?" Her tiny brow wrinkled. "I remember crawling up this branch—and then a strange darkness came over me. I was alone in the dark for a long time. And now . . . now I don't feel the same as I did before." She peered back at her wings again. "Who am I?"

Owl hopped to a branch near the newcomer. "Yes," he said. "You have indeed changed. You are a brand-new creature now. You are called Butterfly."

All afternoon, Butterfly tried out her new wings. She fluttered here and there around the Glen, gaining confidence in her newfound ability to fly as she explored her home. "It all looks so different from the air," she murmured.

As she flitted from branch to twig to leaf, she noticed a group of animals watching her from one end of the Glen. With a ruffle of her wings, she flew over to make their acquaintance. While she was still in the air, however, she heard their voices.

"Kind of skinny, isn't she?" Mouse squeaked.

"Doesn't stay in one place too long," snickered Snail.

"I say there's simply not enough yellow on those wings of hers," buzzed Bee.

"She's definitely lazy," added Ant. "Why, she hasn't done a bit of work all afternoon."

Butterfly cringed. She let her wings carry her past the group of animals, and she pretended she hadn't heard. But for the rest of the afternoon, she brooded over their words.

Tale One: The I Manifesting Itself

She didn't want to be skinny or lazy; she hadn't realized her wings weren't yellow enough or that she was flitting around too much. More than anything else, she wanted the other animals to like her. But Mouse, Snail, Bee, and Ant all thought there was something wrong with her. Finally, with a deep breath, she resolved to become exactly what they wanted her to be.

She ate and ate, until her slender body grew round and heavy. Her wings could no longer carry her gracefully through the air; in fact, they could barely lift her off the ground. This way, she reminded herself, she could more easily stay in one place, just as Snail had wanted. Next, to please Bee, she applied layers of thick yellow paint to her wings, until not a single streak of orange or black showed through. For Ant's benefit, she signed up for Glen cleaning, hoping the work would at least give her a reason to fly again—but it was all groundwork. She crawled back and forth on her short legs, struggling with loads of dirt and dust, feeling small and weak and worthless.

At last, fat, tired, painted, and grounded, she found herself at the Crystal Pool, where the Indigo Wizard lived. The old man sat under the Ancient Oak, playing his flute while the breeze stirred the long, blue strands of his beard.

The sound of his gentle melody lured Butterfly closer. With one last exhausted flutter, she landed on his flute and peered into his face. What she saw there made her burst into tears.

The Wizard took the flute from his lips. "Who are you?"

"I don't know." Butterfly looked up at the tip of his blue hood, then met his gentle eyes. "I used to be a crawler. But then a great darkness came over me, and now I have wings. I am trying to change, so that Snail, Bee, Mouse, and Ant will like me."

"Why?" asked the Wizard.

"Because I want to be accepted here in the Glen."

"But you are not happy, are you?"

Butterfly hung her head. "No," she whispered.

"You have not been true to the Real Change in the darkness," the Wizard said. "Have you?"

Hope stirred in Butterfly's heart. "Can you help me? Can you bring me back to the Real Change?"

"I can guide you to the door," said the Wizard, "but you must go in by yourself and get the Change you seek. Only then will it be real. Come." He carried Butterfly closer to the Crystal Pool. "See your reflection?"

Butterfly peered down at the fat painted creature looking back at her from the still water. "Yes."

The Wizard's hand brought her lower, nearer to the water. "Look more closely. Find your eye. Then look deep within. I will wait for you and hold you safe."

For three days and three nights, the Indigo Wizard held Butterfly in his hand over the Crystal Pool. Butterfly looked deep. . .

Then deeper. . .

And deeper. . .

And all the while, the Wizard held her gently in his hands and did not let her fall.

Then it happened. Change curled through Butterfly and burst out of her. Paint peeled off in layers until her wings were once more paper-light. She lifted up from the Wizard's hands as easily as a breeze and landed on his shoulder.

Tale One: The I Manifesting Itself

He turned his head and smiled at her. "Welcome back. Who are you?"

"I am Beauty." Butterfly kissed the Wizard's cheek. "And Beauty is me."

The last the Wizard saw of her, she was being Beauty all over the Glen.

Open hands

he just showed up one morning. The sun had not yet
dried the Glen's dew, and there he stood: tall, his hands
stuffed into his pockets. At first glance, he seemed much
smaller than he really was.

The Glen animals watched him from their small refuges. Bright eyes peered
out of the crevices of earth and leaf and wood, waiting to see who he was.

Fawn gathered up her courage and made the first move. "Good Food
to you!"

The man scratched his chin. "That's a strange way to say 'good morning.'"

"Mornings are always good," Fawn answered. "It's food I wish for you,
stranger." Fawn took a step closer to the man. "Are you hungry? I can show
you where all Food lives."

The man's lips tightened with suppressed laughter, but his eyes narrowed, as though he were assessing the possibilities. He shrugged. "All right. Show me."

Fawn led the man to the Crystal Pool, where the Indigo Wizard had lived as long as most of the animals could remember. There they found that Rabbit and Fox had run ahead and were waiting to meet the stranger. Sunlight danced on the water; the Wind breathed and sang through the trees; and the Ancient Oak reached its gnarled branches toward the sky. The man looked around him, as though he were uncertain what to expect.

"Good Food to you," said Joyhopper, the rabbit.

"Good Food to you," said Fox.

"What's your name?" asked Fawn.

The man looked from one animal to the other. "I am called Stuck." His voice was deep and gruff. "Alan Stuck."

The rabbit hopped up to the man. "I am Joyhopper. We were just about to eat breakfast. Would you like to join us? We feed here where all Food lives."

Alan Stuck looked around him. Clearly, he saw nothing but the light on the water, the trees stretching upward, the flower-strewn grass. . . .

"Not there! It's here!" Joyhopper waved a paw at the Pool. "The secret's in the Pool, the Crystal Pool."

Alan followed the animals to the water's edge. They looked down into the clear Pool for a moment, while the Wind hummed, and light and water danced together. Then Fawn and Joyhopper moved still closer to the water. They looked first into each other's eyes, then into the Pool.

"Good Food of sweet grass to you, Fawn."

"Good Food of young carrots to you, Joyhopper."

The Wind grew louder, like great feathery wings beating over the water— and then a bunch of young carrots lay on the grass in front of Joyhopper's

16

paws. Fawn bent her head and nosed a pile of sweet grass that hadn't been there a second earlier.

"Ahh," sighed the other animals, who were watching from the trees.

Alan Stuck seemed frozen with amazement. "I've found treasure!" he whispered. "It's mine." He lurched closer to the Pool and leaned over it. "Jewels!" he commanded.

The Wind was quiet in the trees.

"Gold!" Alan's voice was louder now.

The water lay resting in the sun.

"Steak with all the trimmings!" he shouted.

Air and light and water offered nothing.

"Oh my," whispered the animals. "No wonder he is called Alan Stuck."

"He's stuck all right," said first one and then another. "Very stuck."

"He needs the Indigo Wizard," said yet another.

"Yes," they each agreed. "He needs the Wizard."

As soon as the desire sprang from their hearts to their lips, the old man with the long blue beard stepped out from behind the Ancient Oak. His tall blue cap tilted forward as he nodded a greeting. "Good Food to you."

Alan Stuck looked into the Wizard's face—and slowly, his own expression changed. Time seemed to hang waiting while he met the old man's gaze. Little by little, all the greedy eagerness faded from Alan's features, leaving shame and confusion in their place. "I see," he said slowly, "I see that I— I only wanted— You see . . . Oh, I just wanted . . . to be rich, to have what I wanted . . . but now I see."

"What do you see?" the Wizard asked.

Alan hung his head. "I've gone astray. I . . . what I wanted . . . it wasn't right somehow." His shoulders slumped, and he could no longer meet the Wizard's eyes.

"Do not be ashamed, Alan Stuck," the Wizard said. "Do not sink down into guilt." He lifted Alan's head with his hand. "All desires flow from the good. But you have forgotten the truth behind desire."

Alan once more returned the Indigo Wizard's gaze, and his expression slowly cleared. "Please, Wizard," he said, "help me remember. Show me what I have forgotten—this truth you speak of."

"I can only guide you, Alan Stuck. You must be the one to remember." The Wizard took another step closer to Alan. "Take your hands out of your pockets."

Alan pulled out his hands and held them toward the Wizard—but his fingers were curled tight in fists.

"Open your hands, Alan Stuck."

For a moment, it seemed that Alan would not—could not—obey. Then he sighed. His fingers slowly opened.

"Good," the Wizard said. "Now, Alan, look into the Pool and see yourself."

Alan leaned over the water. His own reflection looked back at him.

"Find the center of your eye," the old man said. "Look there until you go deeper, then deeper still. We will wait for you."

The animals came out of the woods and settled in a circle around the Pool. Curled up on the Earth, with the sun's touch warm on their backs, they waited for Alan.

Finally, as the sun was slipping down behind the trees, Alan turned his head toward the Indigo Wizard and the animals.

"Well?" the Wizard asked. "What do you remember?"

"The nature of desire is to flow in and out." Alan smiled. "And it is good."

The old man nodded. "The knowing is the first step, Alan Stuck. The second step is to live what you know."

Alan gazed for a moment at the water, breathing in, breathing out. Then he turned to Joyhopper. "Will you feed with me, my friend?"

"Oh yes, Alan Stuck."

Rabbit and Alan turned back to the Crystal Pool. Then they looked at each other, each reading the other's heart's desire.

"Good Food to you, Alan Stuck."

"Good Food to you, Joyhopper."

They smiled and looked down again at the Pool. Wind breathed through the trees' branches. The water stirred . . .

And an enormous head of lettuce rolled to rest by Joyhopper's paws.

Meanwhile, Alan stared down at a gold medallion at his feet. Letters twined across the gleaming surface: "Alan Un-Stuck," he read out loud.

Joyhopper gave a leap that bumped his head against Fawn's chin. The other animals laughed, and the birds sang their evening song until the Wind could no longer make itself heard above their voices.

"Very good, Alan Un-Stuck," said the Wizard.

And on that spring day, Alan began his apprenticeship with the Indigo Wizard.

The Small Golden Ring

No one had expected this. The surprise was so great that the animals went rushing to the Crystal Pool. They had to see for themselves.

"When did this begin?" asked Snake.

"This morning," replied Grasshopper.

"Right after Good Food time," added Fawn.

"Who was she feeding with?"

"The Wizard," Joyhopper told them.

"Ohh," said the others. They weren't sure what that meant; they only knew it meant something. They looked up into the bright air above the Pool, their eyes fixed on one of the strangest sights they'd ever seen.

Bear floated above the Pool as though she were suspended on a string.

"What's she saying?" asked Snake.

21

The other animals could only shrug, their foreheads wrinkled. Sounds were coming from Bear's mouth, and they sounded like words—but they weren't words they could understand.

"What did the Wizard do?" asked Squirrel.

"He just smiled," said Joyhopper. "And then he left. And Bear has been like this ever since."

"Should we do something?" Fox wondered.

"Could we talk her down, do you think?" put in Squirrel.

"Robin is up there now," Joyhopper told them. "She's perched on Bear's ear, talking to her. We're waiting for her to come tell us what's happening."

The animals sat down, but they could not take their eyes from Bear. It didn't seem right for her to be up there like that, floating in circles above their heads.

"It's not as if she's a cloud," muttered Grasshopper.

"Or a butterfly," added Butterfly.

"I'm worried," said Fawn.

The rest of them nodded, and then they sighed. They leaned back and watched and waited. And waited.

After an hour or so, Robin fluttered down to the ground. "Something wonderful is happening to Bear!" she chirped in a flurry. "The Sun is shining out of her eyes. Strange words are coming from her mouth. I can tell she knows me—but we can't understand each other. Something wonderful is happening!"

The other animals sucked in a deep breath of awe. But they were still puzzled, and they were still worried. They hunkered down on the ground to wait for the Wizard.

As night fell, their eyes filled with wonder. In the darkness, Bear was shining as bright as daylight. She gleamed with such a strange new glow that the familiar Glen seemed different somehow, as though they had never seen it before.

Tale Three: The Small Golden Ring

As the night of light and wonder passed, the animals did not sleep. They stayed by the Pool and waited. They waited for the Indigo Wizard to tell them what was happening.

Just as the sun rose, the Wizard came to them, playing a song on his flute they had never heard before. As he stepped toward them across the grass, his feet fell so gently the grass seemed to giggle, as though his footsteps tickled and made it giddy with relief that he was back. The animals smiled. Everyone was happy near the Indigo Wizard. What had seemed worrisome before now seemed merely joyful.

"Something wonderful is happening to Bear!" shouted Joyhopper.

"But we don't know how to get her down," said Robin.

Bee buzzed up and then down in the air. "She doesn't speak like us now that she's up there."

"Hmm," said the Wizard, stroking his long blue beard. He tipped his head up toward Bear and smiled. "Yes indeed. Well, I can see something wonderful has happened. I will need all your help to bring her down to earth."

"We can help!" The animals huddled around the Wizard, eager to do something for their friend. "Tell us what to do!"

The Wizard waved his hand; a flash lit the air; and then they saw on the ground before them a golden ring.

"Now I will need to teach you a song," the Wizard said.

From air to earth
From thought to thing
It's time to enter
The Small Golden Ring.

The animals looked up at Bear. Then together they sang the Wizard's song.
"She's coming down," Bee buzzed.
"Shh!" said Joyhopper. "Keep singing!"
But Bee was right. Bear had begun to descend. Like a balloon that has lost its air, she spiraled downward in smaller, tighter curves. All the while, the Wizard and the animals continued their chant:

From air to earth,
From thought to thing,
It's time to enter
The Small Golden Ring.

As Bear came closer to the ground, the glow faded from her body. Her eyes no longer shone like the sun. And when she spoke out loud, the others knew she had forgotten the sky language she'd been speaking. "Oh my!" she said.
With a *thump!* she landed, smack in the middle of the Small Golden Ring. All the animals threw themselves on her. "Welcome back!" They hugged her and kissed her. Bee came buzzing up with honey to help Bear regain her strength.
When at last the animals were calmer, Bear looked at the Wizard. The old man looked back at her. Huge tears welled up in Bear's eyes. "Thank you, Wizard."
The Wizard put out his hand to Bear. "What do you know now, Bear?"
Bear heaved an enormous sigh. "I know the Whole that I am part of."
"And do you cry because you are sad?"
Bear lumbered to her feet. "I have no words for what I know. I cannot explain to my friends what happened to me."
"You have been in the Large Golden Ring, where you have seen the Whole," said the Wizard, and then he pointed to the Small Golden Ring. "Bear, there is

the secret of language, the Small Golden Ring. It is the great translator for the Whole. It is magic. Inside this Ring you will discover how to bring air to earth, idea to form, thought to word. You will be able to teach others about the Large Golden Ring you saw while you were in the sky."

Bear turned her big head toward the other animals. Their eager dark eyes were waiting to hear what she would say.

"Please, Bear," said Snake. "What was it like for you up there?"

"What did you see as you were twirling around like a balloon?" asked Fox.

"Tell us," begged Joyhopper. "Try."

Bear looked at the Wizard. The Wizard looked at Bear.

"I will try, Wizard," Bear said. "I will sit in the Small Golden Ring and talk to my friends. I will try to explain to them about the Whole where we all belong, about the Great Golden Circle that is over our heads."

The other animals smiled and sighed. They settled back on the ground and waited for her to speak.

Before she began, though, Bear turned once more to the Wizard. "Wizard?"

"Yes, Bear?"

"I cannot talk to them all the time. I will need to spend more time in my cave, inside the Small Golden Ring. Otherwise, I will have nothing to share with the Glen."

The old man nodded. "I understand."

As he walked away, he could hear Bear saying, "I have a story to tell you."

"Can I sit on your lap?" croaked Frog.

"Can you draw us a picture?" asked Joyhopper.

The Wizard smiled. A new teacher had come to the Glen.

The Source

n a cloudy afternoon in the Glen, Badger crouched at the Indigo Wizard's feet, watching him pack his flute, blanket, and blue cap. "Where are you going, Wizard?" Badger asked.

"I am going to the place where I live," the Wizard replied.

"But you live here, in the Glen, by the Pool."

Wizard searched Badger's eyes; he seemed to be judging how much Badger was ready to hear. "Well, yes—and no."

Badger's ears twitched, and his nose wiggled as he caught the scent of mystery. "Please take me with you! I want to see where you live. I won't be any trouble. I don't even need a blanket. Please, please take me with you!" After knowing the Wizard for the entire three years of his life, Badger had learned

27

that once he had seized the Wizard's attention with a question, he could hold on to it by pleading to know more.

"Whoa! I do believe I am being badgered by Badger." The Wizard laughed. "Well, it does look to me as if you are ready for your first journey to where you live."

"What? Where I live? I live here, in the Glen. I thought you said you were going where you live."

"So I did, Badger, so I did." The Wizard's eyes twinkled as he watched Badger sit up straight on his haunches. "Hmm, who has whose attention now?"

"What do you mean, Wizard?" Badger snuffled at the scent of adventure that hung in the air. "Do I have another home I don't know about? Show me, Wizard—show me where we live!"

"Well then," the old man said as he shut the door of the Ancient Oak, "off we go." He slung his pack over his shoulder and lifted Badger into his arms. After all, the striped animal was only three, and this was his very first journey.

Frog looked up and saw Badger riding on Wizard's shoulder, asking a hundred questions. The Wizard was laughing and stroking Badger's fur as he walked.

"I wonder where they're going," Frog mused. He hopped over to Bear, who was sitting in the Small Golden Ring, telling a story to Fawn. "Bear, where do you think they're going?"

Bear looked up at the sky and scratched her jowl. "Well, Frog, if Badger is with the Wizard, then he is ready for wherever he is going. All I can say for sure is that something wonderful will happen. We will just have to wait and see."

Frog wriggled his long legs and then gave a little hop. "All right, but in the meantime, I'm going to tell everyone in the Glen. That way I won't have to wait alone!" And off he went to spread the news.

Tale Four: The Source

Wizard and Badger had been walking a long time when Badger noticed he was feeling something he'd never experienced before— a special happiness that was a combination of contentment and expectation. He leaned his head against the Wizard and lulled by the old man's steady steps, he floated away into a dream.

In the dream, he was in a boat, sailing upstream. He looked down and realized that the boat was the Wizard, and the Wizard was the boat. With complete certainty, Badger knew he was utterly safe; he could venture anywhere in this boat with no fear that it would ever capsize or go adrift.

"Badger, wake up!"

The voice penetrated his dream, and Badger stirred.

"Badger, wake up!"

Badger wiggled and tried to open his eyes.

"Badger, wake up!"

Badger sat bolt upright on the Wizard's shoulder. Wide awake now, he realized he was seeing the world with a new clarity. Every detail shone as though dipped in gold; every sound stood out distinct from all other sounds; each of his senses was sharper than ever before. He felt as though he might even have a few new senses he'd never realized he possessed.

When he tipped back his head, he saw the gold light that bathed the world shone down from a huge cavern above them. Like a glimmering river that danced with rainbows, the light flowed into the Glen far below, and there it fed into the Crystal Pool.

He let out a long sigh. "This must be the home where all Food lives."

"Well said, Badger, well said." The Wizard stroked Badger's head. "What else do you know?"

A sound caught Badger's attention. The more he heard it, the more his heart filled with love. Light flowed out from him like water—and the more love he felt, the greater was the rainbow-shot river that poured down to the Crystal Pool. All the while, the sound beat inside him, a constant rhythm that filled him with still stronger love.

"Oh, Wizard! The sound!" Knowledge swept over Badger. "The sound is the Heart! That is what I know. I know that you and I live in the Heartland. We come from the Heartland. This is our home."

The Wizard's hand cupped the Badger's head, and light spilled in a wash of gold from them to the Glen below.

After a long moment, Badger sighed. "Can we come here again, Wizard?"

The Wizard stroked Badger's silky ears. "You never leave here, Badger. You are always here. You forgot that for a while, but now you are ready to remember. Now you can come and go whenever you like. When you come, you feed yourself. When you go, you feed others."

Badger's furry head furrowed with puzzled wrinkles. "But Wizard, you are other and I am self, and yet we are here together in the Heartland."

The Wizard laughed in delight. "So what do you know now, Badger?"

"I know how to get home, Wizard, to the place where I also live, back in the Glen."

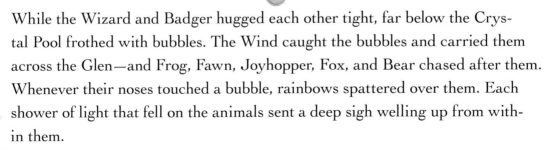

While the Wizard and Badger hugged each other tight, far below the Crystal Pool frothed with bubbles. The Wind caught the bubbles and carried them across the Glen—and Frog, Fawn, Joyhopper, Fox, and Bear chased after them. Whenever their noses touched a bubble, rainbows spattered over them. Each shower of light that fell on the animals sent a deep sigh welling up from within them.

"Something wonderful is happening—to Badger, and to us," they said to each other.

Because of Badger's experiences that day, not only Badger was growing in his awareness of the Wizard and the Heartland: they all were, all the animals of the Glen. And thereafter, the animals spoke of this time as the Feast of Rainbow Bubbles.

Rejuvenation

I do so know how to play!"
"You do not!"
"I do so!"
"Do not!"

The argument between Ant and Bee had been going on for more than three hours.

"They're getting nowhere," said Robin.

Fawn nodded. "They're just repeating themselves over and over. It's like they're caught in a trap."

"That's not good for any of us. We'd better call a meeting to help them—and the rest of the Glen."

The Awakening Tales

Noon was a good time for a Glen meeting, Owl always said—so the animals gathered when the sun was at the top of the sky. All the animals—Squirrel, Frog, Ant, Bee, Owl, Bear, Joyhopper, Butterfly, Snail, Fox, Turtle, Badger, Wolf, Mrs. Duck and her brood, Fawn, and Robin—met under the Ancient Oak beside the Crystal Pool.

Owl convened the meeting. "Hear ye, hear ye! The Glen community has gathered to help resolve the stalemate between party number-one, Mr. Ant, and party number-two, Mrs. Bee. Let us first hear from Mrs. Bee."

Bee buzzed into the middle of the gathering. "Ant says I always work and never play. He says my buzzing is obnoxious because it never stops. He says I work so much that I upset the Glen's balance. But playing is childish. I'm too grown up for that, and I don't have time."

"Thank you, Mrs. Bee," said Owl. "Very nicely worded. Very succinct." He turned toward Ant. "Next!"

Ant worked his way to the center of the circle. "She doesn't play," he said. "She never rests. She's always buzzing around. We ants at least have picnics. Everyone needs to relax sometimes. What I told her was for her own good—and for the good of the Glen."

Ant looked smug; Bee looked indignant; and the other animals looked baffled. Fox's forehead was wrinkled, Turtle scratched his chin, and Joyhopper's nose twitched in bewilderment. Even Bear could find no words, and Badger's eyes filled with sadness as he gazed at Bee and Ant. *We need the Wizard,* was the thought that sprang into each animal's mind.

As soon as the thought entered their heads, the Wizard appeared. He was jump-roping across the Glen, singing opera at the top of his lungs. A huge sack bounced on his back as he came toward them.

"This," said Bear, "is going to be a very interesting meeting."

Tale Five: Rejuvenation

Once the old man had reached the circle of animals and had stopped singing, Owl summarized the proceedings for him. "We appear to be at a stalemate," Owl concluded. "We need your expertise."

Everyone nodded and felt grateful that Owl was so educated and used such big words.

With the jump rope hanging from one hand, the Wizard stroked his beard with the other.

Ant wiggled with impatience. "I'm right, aren't I, Wizard? And Bee is wrong."

Bee gave a little buzz. "No! I'm right, Wizard! Ant is wrong, isn't he?"

There was nothing but silence after they spoke. Bee and Ant seemed stuck in the silence, like insects caught in amber. Silence . . .

Silence . . .

Silence.

No one in the assembly said anything.

After a moment, Wizard shifted the sack off his shoulder. He bent over it and began placing its contents one-by-one on the ground. The animals pressed closer to see, murmuring to each other as their curiosity dispelled the heavy silence.

"Look!" exclaimed Fox. "Four little roller skates." He grabbed them and put them on his paws. "Now I can skate all over the Glen! Bet you can't catch me, Joyhopper!"

"Oh yeah?" Joyhopper reached for a skateboard just his size. A second later, Fox and Joyhopper were rolling off across the Glen.

Meanwhile, Owl was setting out a game of chess and had invited Frog to join him. Before long, Turtle and Squirrel were sharing jacks, Badger was scribbling with a box of crayons and a pad of paper, and the ducklings had

seven yo-yos gliding up and down. Fawn and Wolf were playing badminton.

Only Ant, Bee, and the Wizard still stood silent.

The Wizard bent down. "Why aren't you playing with the others?"

Ant and Bee looked around the Glen at everyone laughing and enjoying themselves.

Bee gave a tiny buzz. "Um, well . . . you see, Wizard, I don't really know how to play. I buzz around, you know, and I'm awfully busy, and I . . . well, I—uh . . ." Her voice trailed away, and she sighed. "I guess Ant was right. Now that I see how happy everyone is . . . well, I realize I've been missing out on something. I guess maybe we need to act like children sometimes." For a moment, she watched the others playing, and then she turned back to Ant. "It looks like playing is good for the Glen after all. Will you teach me how to play, Ant, the way you do at your picnics?"

Ant gazed back at Bee. He shifted his feelers back and forth, he glanced at the Wizard, then he looked down at his feet. "Well . . . mmm . . . well, I guess I wasn't being too truthful, Bee. I don't really go to picnics to play. I work at picnics, the same way I do the rest of the time. I saw things I didn't like about you . . . but they were really things I don't like about myself. I'm sorry, Bee. I'm afraid I don't know how to play."

Bee smiled at Ant. "I'm sorry too, Ant." She turned to the Wizard. "Is there anything left in your sack for us? Something that would help us learn to play?"

"Let's see." The old man reached deep inside the sack and groped around. "There's just one toy left." He pulled out a small, two-seater airplane. Ant and Bee gave a sigh of disappointment: the propeller was broken.

But then they looked at each other and burst into laughter as the same thought occurred to them both. Ant jumped into the back seat and Bee took

the front. Bee turned around and used her wings instead of a propeller. The Wizard laughed as they took off, yelling into the Wind, and then he picked up his jump rope and began to sing.

Later that night, as the animals made their way to their beds, they realized they were more relaxed and refreshed than they had been in a long time.

And ever since, the Glen celebrates the Festival of Young-Making in the Season of Rejuvenation.

Caretaking

The people came to the Glen with a picnic basket, a black box, and several canvas bags. The black box was making loud noises.

"Oh good," Ant said, "a picnic! Tell the others."

"Wait," said Owl. "We don't know what kind they are. Don't venture out too soon."

The animals hid and watched the intruders.

The two young ones were already fighting over their food. They yelled and pushed, pulled and hit, while the older ones sat and laughed. "They're just children," the woman said. "Let them get it out of their systems."

Fox winced. The noises from the black box combined with the children's voices and hurt his ears.

"Why do they act like that?" asked Badger.

Squirrel shrugged, his tiny brow furrowed.

As the animals watched, the children yanked handfuls of flowers and leaves from the earth, roots and all. They brought fistfuls back to the woman.

"Look, George, aren't they sweet?" she cooed.

The man was too busy throwing empty cans at Tree to answer. "Bull's-eye!" he shouted.

"Run along, kids," the woman said. "You go off and play. Mommy's going to relax."

The animals saw one child take a little knife and carve lines deep into Tree. The other child had found Spider in her web. "Ew! A spider! Let's get it."

The children grabbed matches from one of the canvas bags and lit the web. Spider struggled to escape, but the flames took her and her web away from the Glen forever.

The children laughed and began looking for something else to do.

As the sun sank behind the trees, the people finally left the Glen. The animals waited a moment, still hidden, and then they heaved sighs of relief. They crept out and surveyed the damage.

Cans were everywhere. Papers and food were strewn across the ground. Flowers lay wilting. Tree was bleeding. And Spider was gone forever.

No one could find anything to say.

Finally, Owl broke the silence. "We better find the Wizard."

The old man was on the ground under the Ancient Oak. Tufts of his blue hair had been pulled from his head, leaving raw places behind. Blood dripped from a deep gash in his leg. One eyebrow had been singed away, leaving a charred mark the shape of a spider. Gold tears spilled out of his eyes and across his cheeks.

Fawn leaned down and licked the wound in the Wizard's leg. Joyhopper gathered up the strands of gleaming hair and tried to press them back into place on the Wizard's head. The other animals stared at the burned eyebrow and wondered how they could help him.

"Wizard! Tell us what to do, Wizard!" begged Joyhopper.

"Heal the Glen," the Wizard whispered. "Heal the Glen."

Badger was the first to understood what the Wizard meant. "Quick! Gather up his tears and follow me!"

The animals put out their paws to catch the golden liquid, but a gruff voice they seldom heard interrupted them. "Take my leaves," the Ancient Oak said. A branch creaked down low enough for them to reach. "Use my leaves to collect the tears."

The animals carefully picked only the leaves they needed to catch the Wizard's golden tears. Then, carrying the tears, they followed Badger across the Glen.

Fox spilled the golden liquid he carried into Tree's deep wound. "Ahh," Tree whispered as her torn bark grew back together. "Thank you."

Squirrel patted the flowers into the ground, and Joyhopper dripped gold over their wilted petals. "Ahh," they sighed and stood up straighter. "Thank you."

Badger turned to Spider—but when the tears fell on her charred body, nothing happened. The animals shed tears of their own now, for they loved Spider. Then Snail noticed something: a single tear had penetrated the clump of scorched remains—and from it tumbled a tiny fluff ball. "Look!" Snail cried. As the animals watched, the ball of fluff burst open, and hundreds of baby spiders crawled out of it.

"Spider's children!" The animals smiled through their tears. "The children have survived. Now we will always have a part of their mother with us."

Next, the animals scurried to gather up every can and paper that littered the Glen. They buried it all, even the crumbs of food, for Ant did not want to partake of such things. "Bury it deep," Badger instructed as he helped to dig the hole with his powerful claws. "Deeper, deeper, deeper."

The animals pushed all the torn bits, the empty cans, the scattered food into the hole and covered it with good clean earth. They spilled the last of the Indigo Wizard's tears from the oak leaves onto the ground. Tiny shoots of green sprang from the soil as they watched.

The moon had risen by the time they returned to the Wizard. They found him humming as he sat beside the shining Crystal Pool. His blue hair was once more smooth, and his leg was clearly as good as new, though the animals could still see a trace of a scar. Relief filled their hearts with joy as they ran to hug him.

"Oh, Wizard! Who were those people who came to the Glen?"

The old man smiled down at the animals, and then he wrapped his arms around them all. "They were the unawake, my friends."

Tale Six: Caretaking

The animals pushed closer to the Wizard's warmth. All that night, they stayed near to him beside the Crystal Pool.

Mirrors

urry up, Snail! At this rate, we'll never get to the Crystal Pool."

"Turtle, I'm going as fast as I can."

Turtle sighed. "Well, hop on my back then. I'll give you a ride."

Snail crawled onto Turtle's back, and Turtle walked at his quickest pace. They'd gone about six inches, when Bear lumbered up to them. "Hurry up, you two! The Wizard will be there soon."

Turtle tried to crawl faster. "I'm walking as quickly as I can," he panted. "You'll just have to tell him we're on our way."

Bear bent down and picked up Turtle and Snail. "I'll carry you both. And then we'll all arrive together."

Everyone but the Wizard was already there when they reached the Crystal Pool. Excitement surged through the animals, for today was a special day, the Day of Truth-Seeing, when the Indigo Wizard told them a story about himself. This year, Alan Unstuck was with them as the Wizard's apprentice. Joyhopper was in Alan's lap; Bee buzzed over his head; and Butterfly fluttered back and forth on her orange wings. The other animals stirred restlessly, waiting for the Wizard.

And then the Crystal Pool began to bubble. "Look!" Turtle whispered to Snail, and out stepped the Indigo Wizard, as dry as if he had come from the Ancient Oak instead of the Pool.

The animals sighed with joy and love. They knew that when the Indigo Wizard came to the Glen, he had changed them all. He had taught them about the Inner Sun, the Light that shone not only inside himself but inside each of the creatures as well. Because of the Wizard, they were learning to know the Light, and at moments like this, when the Wizard came to them, their love filled the entire Glen so that even the Wind fell silent. They nudged each other closer together, making room for the old man to join their circle.

"What story will you tell us this year, Wizard?" Fawn asked.

The Wizard smiled. "Would you like to hear how I became indigo?"

"Weren't you always indigo?" Mouse squeaked.

The Wizard shook his head. Snail's mouth fell open in surprise; how could the Wizard not have been indigo and still have been the Wizard? She looked at Turtle to see if he would know the answer, but Turtle only turned to Frog, and Frog looked at Bear. Bear shrugged and waved her paw toward the Wizard, reminding them all that the Wizard would answer their questions. The animals

turned back toward the Wizard, pushing so close to him that Turtle, Snail, Badger, Frog, Grasshopper, and Mouse all ended up in Bear's lap. Everyone wanted to be as near as possible to the Wizard so they'd hear every single word.

The Wizard leaned back on his hands, and the Wind stirred his blue hair. "Well, let's see, where should I start? All of you remember where I came from?"

The animals nodded. "The Great Mountain of the Inner Sun," said Badger.

"That's right. I came from the Inner Sun, and his light lives in me, just as I live in the Inner Sun. But when I first came to this land, I had much to remember about who I am. My time here was my apprenticeship, for although the Always-Sun was in me, I lived now in your land's time. The story I am about to tell you happened in the ninetieth year of my apprenticeship. If you had met me then, you would have seen all the colors of the sunrise in my hair and skin."

Turtle scratched his head, and Bear wrinkled her forehead; they were trying to imagine what the Wizard would have looked like. Would his hair have shone gold like the dawn's first light? Would his skin have glimmered, all purple and rose and pearly like morning clouds?

"That was the year," the Wizard continued, "I met the Lumens. They were nomads who followed the Sun of the Outer Sky. The Lumens traveled from north to south and then from south to north, following the tilt of the Earth toward the sun, so that they would always be as close as possible to the light that shines on the Outer World. The Lumens were like prisms that catch light and break it into colors, so that each Lumen was a different color, one red, one yellow, another purple, and yet another green. Each glowed with her own reflection of the light. Torque was one of the Lumens, and when the light hit her skin and hair, she shone indigo blue."

"Indigo!" The animals whispered the word to each other, their eyes round. They wiggled on their haunches, as though they had all suddenly found they were sitting on something sharp and hard. How could this Torque have been the color the Wizard was now? "That can't be true," whispered Frog, but the other animals nudged him to be silent. They knew that even if what the Wizard told them was hard to understand, it was always true.

The Wizard smiled at them as though he knew their thoughts, and then he continued with his story. "Torque and I began to tell each other about ourselves—but the more we talked, the more angry with me she became."

"Angry!" squeaked Mouse. "What right had she to be angry with you?"

"Well, you see, I spoke to her of the Inner Sun, the Light that shines through me. But Torque knew only the light from the sun of the Outer Sky. That sun," the Wizard pointed with his hand toward the sky, "was the light she loved. It was the light she followed, traveling from north to south and south to north, in order to be always as close as possible to it. She laughed when I spoke to her of the Inner Sun. 'If your Great Inner Sun even exists,' she said, 'then he is locked inside you. How can he have any power? Not like my sun, the Real Light that gives life to all the Earth. He is what makes me shine blue.'"

Mouse stamped her tiny foot. "I don't like Torque. She's stupid! Why, she only knows how to use her outside eyes! She doesn't even know she can look inside and see."

"That's right," Snail said. "Her Great Sun is always moving around. It's not like the Inner Sun."

"Only a silly person would think the Outer Sun could have the same power as the Inner Sun." Scorn dripped from Wolf's voice. "A silly person or a bad person."

The animals pressed even closer, as though they would help protect the Wizard from Torque. Only Alan was silent as the animals clamored to defend the Wizard they loved so much.

"She must be bad." Mouse's shrill little voice rose above the other animals'. "If I ever run into her, I know I won't like her. She's not like us. She doesn't know the Inner Sun."

"But she was indigo blue," Bear said softly.

"Well, then," Frog snapped, "I don't like blue. I don't like anything about this Torque."

"But Frog," Bear said, "the Wizard is blue now."

The animals fell silent. They turned back to the Wizard. "What do you think happened next?" he asked them.

"Did you use your power to teach her a lesson?" Frog asked. "Did you wave your hand and make her disappear?"

"Yes!" Mouse punched the air with her tiny fist, and her tail twitched in circles. Alan smiled at her.

The Wizard smiled too. "No, I did not. But something else happened instead."

Mouse gave a sigh of disappointment.

"What happened, Wizard?" asked Snail.

"The Inner Sun was suddenly there, shining beside me. 'What are you doing?' the Sun asked me."

Mouse climbed off Bear's knee and pressed close to the Wizard. "What did you say?"

"Before I could answer, I saw the Great Sun of the Outer Sky come down beside Torque. He asked her the same question: 'What are you doing?' And Torque answered, 'I'm about to show this deluded apprentice the right way to go.'"

"Deluded!" Frog slapped his hands against his knees. "How dare she!" The other animals joined in, their voices rising in a buzz of outrage.

"Let the Wizard tell his story," Alan reminded gently, and the animals fell silent.

"I heard both Suns speak: 'Show each other the truth!'

"So Torque and I stepped close to each other and our eyes locked. I was braced for the clash of her will against mine—but a strange thing happened instead. I saw in Torque's eyes my own reflection—and shining around my image was the Inner Sun. At the same moment, Torque gasped and took a step backward, and I realized she saw in my eyes her own Outer Sun. The look on her face changed, and I knew she could never fight against me now, for she truly loved her sun as much as she loved herself."

"But—" Mouse's tiny face was screwed up as though she were struggling to swallow something sour and unfamiliar. "How could Torque see the Outer Sun in your eyes, Wizard? Shouldn't she have seen the Inner Sun? And how could you see the Inner Sun in *her* eyes?"

"I am the mirror that reflects the Light. And so are you, Mouse." The Wizard touched Mouse's head with the tip of his blue finger. "And you too, Frog, and you, Bear, and each of you. When we look deeply into each other, we see that Light—and then we see that what we thought was separate from ourselves and strange is really just the Light that shines inside our own hearts, the same Light we love."

The Wizard paused, and the animals held their breath, waiting for him to continue with the story. "As we looked into each other's eyes, Torque and I remembered what we had forgotten we knew, and we were both changed forever. When we came back to awareness, I saw that Torque no longer looked the same—her skin and hair shone with all the colors of the sunrise. She still loved the Sun of the Outer Sky, but now she knew that the Outer Sun and the Inner

Sun are one. Meanwhile, she was staring at me in amazement, for I too had changed. Now I was indigo blue."

The Wizard looked around the circle of animals. "And that was the day I became the Indigo Wizard. The Outer and Inner Sun are one in me."

Mouse sighed and stuck out her lip. "But I don't understand. Why did you become indigo, Wizard? It just doesn't make sense!"

The Wizard only smiled, and gradually, the frown on Mouse's face relaxed as she pondered Wizard's story. She turned to Frog and looked into his eyes, curious as to what she might see. Frog looked back at Mouse; Bear looked into Fawn's eyes, and she into Bear's. Turtle's eyes met Snail's; Wolf's met Badger's; Butterfly's met Bee's. Alan Unstuck and the Wizard exchanged glances, and then Alan looked up at the sun above their heads.

Alan smiled.

Resurrection

e gentle with him, Bear."

"I'm trying, Badger."

Bear did her best to make her big paws as soft and light as Butterfly's wings, but Snake still whimpered as she carried him to the edge of the Glen. The others, including the Indigo Wizard, were already there.

"See," said the Wizard, dusting off a rock, "Sky Sun has made it warm for you."

But Snake was moaning too loudly to hear the Wizard's words. This was the first time he had ever died, and he was very scared.

"Does it hurt, Snake?" asked Fox.

"I think so," quavered Snake.

The Wizard slid his finger along Snake's back, but Snake refused to be calmed by the old man's touch. "I don't want to give up my skin!" Snake wailed. "Without my skin, I will die. I like my life, I like my skin. It's beautiful—isn't it beautiful, Wizard? It has stripes of red and orange. I don't want to give it up!"

Snake's terror was contagious, and soon the other animals were wailing too. Their sobs were so loud, and their tears so plentiful, a small pool collected at the base of Snake's rock.

"Wizard," begged Bear, "use your power to stop Snake from dying."

"Very well," said the Wizard.

One by one, the animals stopped sobbing. "Did he say he would?" whispered Joyhopper.

"That's what he said!" said Fox.

Snake's moans quieted, and he lifted his head. The pool of tears at the base of the rock evaporated in the sun's warmth. Butterfly fluttered down and lit on Snake's nose.

The Wizard walked in a circle around Snake. Then he waved his arms above his head. He waltzed a few steps with an invisible partner. He threw back his head and let out a trill of opera.

The animals shifted back and forth uneasily. "I don't think this is going to work," whispered Bear to Badger.

The Indigo Wizard stood still and looked at the animals. "Do you *really* want to know how to not die?"

"Yes!" the animals shouted.

The Wizard leaned over and whispered in Snake's ear. As the animals watched, Snake's breathing became slower and slower. He no longer looked frightened.

Tale Eight: Resurrection

"Is he dying?" asked Joyhopper in a small voice.

"Yes," said the Wizard.

"But—"

"Shh," said the Wizard. "Watch."

Now Snake's breathing was so slow that minutes seemed to go by between each breath. Butterfly flew to the end of the rock to give Snake more room to die. Inch by inch, Snake's beautiful stripes peeled away from him. Little by little, the gold and red colors they had known so well grew dull and dead.

The animals watched and waited.

Three hours later, all that remained of the old Snake was a flimsy pile of dry skin. But at the other end of the rock, where Butterfly still perched, curved a longer, brighter Snake.

"He came back!" cried Fox.

Snake lifted his head and looked at Butterfly. They exchanged a long look, and Butterfly smiled and nodded. Then Snake's gaze shifted from Butterfly to his brighter, bigger body, and then to the Wizard's face. "You were right, Wizard. The only way to *not* die is to die."

"But how can that make sense?" asked Joyhopper. "What happened, Snake?"

"I died, Joyhopper. I just . . . died."

Joyhopper looked from the empty pile of skin to Snake's new scarlet and gold stripes. His furry forehead wrinkled. "What did the Wizard whisper in your ear, Snake?"

Snake stretched his brilliant stripes in the sunlight. "He told me to go to the place where I am not my skin."

The Wizard clapped his hands. "I think it's about time for the funeral!"

Laughing and singing, the animals marched behind the old man as he carried Snake's skin to its burial.

The Large Golden Ring

veryone noticed it. All the animals in the Glen were aware that Ant was no longer the same.

"He's been going on like this since the Festival of Young-Making," said Owl.

The animals looked up at Ant where he sat on the very top leaf of the very highest tree. His flying cap was on his head, and his aviator glasses perched on his nose.

"He's just sitting there," said Turtle. "Just looking at the sky. As though he's waiting for something."

Bear looked up at the tiny figure, and her eyes grew bright with tears. "Oh, Turtle," she said, "he so wants to have wings. You have to understand—when he went up in the airplane with Mrs. Bee, he experienced a great thing. He experienced the Big Sight."

"Is that why he wears those glasses all the time?" asked Frog.

"Probably." Bear sighed. "The glasses help him forget how little he can see now. And they help him to be ready."

"Ready for what?" asked Fawn.

"For another journey."

"But Bear," Joyhopper said, "the airplane's wings broke when Ant and Mrs. Bee landed. Mrs. Bee can't take Ant for another ride."

"I know." A single tear spilled out of Bear's left eye. "I know."

Longing to comfort Bear's tears, the animals huddled closer to her where she sat beside the Small Golden Ring. They did not understand what Ant longed for—but they wished they could do something to help him too.

"What a somber group!" Alan Unstuck exclaimed as he and the Indigo Wizard joined the group of animals.

"We are cogitating very hard," said Owl.

Alan looked as though he were trying not to smile. "Cogitating?"

"With our hearts," replied Turtle.

"Ah," said Alan gravely.

"Then," said the Wizard, "someone must need help."

"Yes, yes!" they shouted together, their hearts lifting.

Everyone scrunched still closer together to make room for the Wizard and Alan in their circle. Once they were all seated again, Owl informed them—at length—of all the details regarding Ant's situation.

An hour later, the Wizard, Alan, and all the animals got to their feet and proceeded together to the tallest tree, where Ant had taken up residence.

Tale Nine: The Large Golden Ring

"Hello up there!" yelled the Wizard.

Ant's voice floated down to them from the top of the tree. "Hi, Wizard."

"Nice view up there, Ant?" the Wizard shouted.

"Yes, Wizard."

The old man scratched his head. "Ant, your voice sounds sad."

A long sigh drifted down to the animals below. "Yes, Wizard."

The Wizard stroked his long blue beard and waited.

After a moment, Bear called, "You don't have the words you need to explain, do you, Ant?"

"No, Bear," replied Ant. "I don't."

"Well then," said Bear, "come down. You know the Wizard makes the sad happy!"

Ant stared off at the sky. He had been so consumed with longing and sadness, he'd forgotten the Wizard would know what to do with the yearning feelings that filled him. This time when he sighed, his tiny shoulders straightened. "I'm coming!" he yelled down at the animals, "but this tree is so high it will take me all day to get there."

Alan laughed. "How about I start up to meet you, Ant?"

Maybe, Joyhopper thought as he watched, *Alan climbs so quickly because Tree is moving her branches closer together to help him.*

By the time Alan reached Ant, Ant had only crawled a few inches from the top of the tree. Alan held out his hand, and Ant crawled onto his fingers, across his palm, and up his arm to his shoulder, where he took a firm hold on Alan's collar.

Alan descended the tree even more quickly than he'd climbed it. When he and Ant were back on the ground, the animals once more formed their circle. Bear placed the Small Golden Ring at the center.

"Sit in the Small Golden Ring, Ant," she invited. "Then you will find the words you need."

Alan gently placed Ant in the center of the Ring. Ant sucked in a breath, and words spilled out of him.

"Oh, Wizard! Oh, friends! My heart hurts! I'm so small, and everything around me is so much bigger than I am. For me to go anywhere in the Glen takes me so long. And I can only see the world around me in tiny glimpses. Instead of seeing all of Bear, I see just the fur on the end of her hind paws. Instead of seeing the Indigo Wizard from head to toe, the way the rest of you see him, I can only see the blue hem of his robe.

"But when Mrs. Bee took me up in the airplane, it was like heaven. I could look down and see the tops of your heads. I could see all of you at once. I saw the entire shape of the Crystal Pool. I saw the leaves that grow at the top of the Ancient Oak. I flew inside the Wind. I . . . I . . . I felt . . ."

For a moment, Ant could only stammer, but then he said: *"High in the air, Ant flies. The small is gone."*

The animals were silent, pondering Ant's words. One by one, they turned their heads toward the Wizard, wondering what he would make of this.

The Wizard smiled. "Well, Ant, it sounds to me as if you have entered the Large Golden Ring—and now you are bringing your new understanding into the Small Golden Ring where it can teach the others."

"But, Wizard," interrupted Bee, "I am always up in the air flying around—and it hasn't affected me the way it has Ant."

"That is because Ant was ready, Mrs. Bee. You take your world for granted, but for Ant, it became the door that opened into the Large Golden Ring. He was ready to experience what lay inside."

Bear looked up at the air above her head, remembering the door the Wizard had helped her open.

"Is the Large Golden Ring the same as the Small Ring, Wizard?" Robin asked.

Tale Nine: The Large Golden Ring

"Yes and no." The Wizard smiled again at the confusion he saw in the animals' eyes. "Bear sits in the Small Golden Ring and tells stories to all the Glen family, teaching you about her experiences inside the Large Golden Ring. What Ant has learned and experienced is different from Bear's experience—but the journey was the same. He too will be able to teach you from the Small Golden Ring all that he learns in the Large Ring."

Mrs. Bee's antenna twitched as she tried to make sense of the Wizard's words.

"You have a great gift, Ant," said Bear. "It is called poetry. It speaks to our hearts and teaches us."

Ant looked into Bear's eyes. "Really?" he whispered.

Bear nodded her big head. "Really, Ant. Try it out again."

Ant sat up straight. He cleared his throat. The other animals waited.

"Riding the Wind, ah! a kiss!"

The animals were silent as Ant's words rang inside their hearts and minds.

"Something wonderful has happened to Ant," whispered Joyhopper.

"But Bear," said Ant, "I still want wings."

Bear looked at the Wizard. He winked at her. Bear nodded and turned back to Ant.

"You can have wings, Ant," she said. "Come to my cave, and I will show you another door into the Large Golden Ring. It is called Dream Time."

"Will I have wings there?" begged Ant.

Bear smiled. "In Dream Time you will find airplanes that have yet to be flown."

Gold streamed from the animals' hearts as they watched Bear carry Ant to her cave. Then they turned their heads and noticed that the Wizard and Alan Unstuck were walking away together. The Wizard put his hand on Alan's shoulder.

"Would you like to go for an airplane ride?" they heard him ask Alan.

Mastery

No one noticed the eagle that soared in lazy, easy circles high over the Glen. Then, silently, as swift as an arrow shot at a target, it dropped. . .

And Joyhopper was gone from them, trapped by Eagle's talons as her great wings carried her higher and higher, back into the cloudless sky.

The other animals saw it happen, but it was over before they could do anything. They stood frozen, looking up at the small shape that dangled beneath Eagle. Ant and Bear were in the Small Golden Ring; Frog was at the Pool; and Fawn, Fox, and Turtle were by the pine tree. None of them could speak.

Alan Unstuck had been planting seedlings at the edge of the meadow when he looked up and saw Joyhopper. "No!" he screamed. He ran beneath Eagle, his arms upstretched, but he was as helpless as the others. At last he stumbled to a stop, and then he shook his fists at the sky. "I'll get you, Eagle!" He choked, as though his throat were full of stones. "I'll get you for this!"

The animals gathered around him. Fawn nudged his hand; Fox rubbed against his leg; but Alan seemed not to notice. He strode out of the Glen, his features twisted in an expression the animals had never seen on his face before.

"Will Joyhopper be all right?" Turtle asked the Wizard later, when the animals had gathered around him by the Crystal Pool.

The Wizard sighed. "We will just have to wait and see."

"He must be ready for this," said Bear. "Otherwise it wouldn't have happened."

"That's right, Bear," Ant agreed. "He must be ready."

The other animals sat silent, taking comfort from these words as they waited.

Then Alan stomped into the circle of creatures, interrupting their quiet. He held a rifle under his arm. "I am going to the high mountain," he announced grimly.

"And what will you do there?" asked the Indigo Wizard.

"I am going to kill Eagle. I am going to make her pay for what she has done to Joyhopper."

The Wizard looked thoughtfully at Alan. "You must do what you must do," the Wizard said at last. "You are the only one with the power to do what you must."

"Right," said Alan. He turned on his heel and strode toward the mountain, his rifle gripped tight in his hand.

The Wizard turned back to the circle of animals. "Shall we do what we can to help him?"

The animals nodded. When the Wizard began to hum, they joined their voices to his. The soft sound filled the air around them. It swirled in ever-

widening circles that spread outward from the Glen and climbed through the air, higher and higher.

By midafternoon, Alan had reached the rocky crevices at the top of the mountain. He searched through them, his anger and sorrow growing, but he found no sign of Eagle. At last, however, he came across an old woman gathering kindling.

"Greetings, stranger," she said.

"Have you seen an eagle?" His voice grated as he pushed it past the rocks that still seemed to fill his throat. "Do you know where she lives?"

"An eagle?" The woman shook her head. "Eagles are rare in these parts." She cocked her head to one side and examined Alan. "Why do you carry a gun?"

Alan shifted the rifle in his hand. "I am going to kill the eagle. She took away my friend."

"I see." The old woman scratched her white eyebrow. "Are you sure your friend is gone?"

"I saw it happen," Alan said. "I saw Eagle take Joyhopper from us."

"Oh, so you *saw* it." The woman nodded her head, and then she pointed up at the sky. "The eagle lives there. Above the clouds. You'll have to look for her there."

"Don't be silly," Alan snapped. "I can't go there, above the clouds."

The woman shrugged. "You can, if you want."

"How?"

The woman raised her brows, as though he had asked a foolish question. "Fly. Of course."

Alan scowled. "I can't fly."

"You can, you know. If you get lighter. When you are light as a feather, the Wind can lift you above the clouds."

"How am I supposed to get lighter?"

The old woman looked at him for a long moment. "You are the only one with the power to do what you must do," she said at last.

Alan stared back at her. "The Wizard said those same to words to me," he said slowly.

The woman nodded.

Alan looked up at the clouds. His body felt heavy, as heavy as a stone. "I cannot make myself light," he said bitterly.

"You have the power to master the heavy, stranger," said the old woman. "You have the power to be master over the heavy."

Alan heard a humming noise then. It seemed to come from both the air around him and from his own bones, from his heart, from within his skull. Strength vibrated through him, and he knew he was ready now. He sat at the woman's feet and waited.

She reached toward him with her gnarled hand and touched him between the eyes. Instantly, an immense cavern yawned in front of him, but he sensed that the cavern was also within his own mind. From the cave's dark depths, he saw anger, hate, vengeance, and delusion staring out at him with fiery eyes, and within his head he heard their screams:

Pick up your gun, the Eagle kill!
You have more power, you have gun skill.
Pluck its feathers, gouge its sight.
Kill the Eagle, show your might!

Alan stared into the darkness for a long moment, and then he shook his head. "No! Those are lies!" He squared his shoulders. "But I will show you my might."

Alan let the humming fill him, and then he opened his mouth and joined his voice to the sound. Gold spilled from his throat.

66

Tale Ten: Mastery

The real is Love; this is true sight.
The Eagle did only teach us right.
I break this gun upon your head,
And shall not grieve when you are dead.

One by one, the gleaming eyes within the cave went dark. Where the cavern had been were only clouds now, and the Wind swirled through them, blowing them away.

Alan looked out from the mountaintop at a clear sky. A sound beside him made him turn toward the woman. She stood beside him, gripping the rocks beneath her with Eagle's talons, her hair a stream of sleek feathers. In her arms, rested Joyhopper. The rabbit lifted his head and wiggled his furry nose.

"And do you see now?" the woman asked Alan.

Alan's heart lifted, as though the sun had risen after a particularly long, dark night. He nodded. "Now I can truly see. Without delusion."

The Indigo Wizard led the solemn ceremony beside the Crystal Pool. Alan had passed his first great test in his apprenticeship, and the animals joined him in celebrating this important moment.

"Alan Unstuck," said the Wizard, "you have passed the Test of Delusion. You had power to do what you must—and you chose to use your power to do what you truly needed to do. True-seeing was your reward." He placed on Alan's head an indigo cap with the emblem of an eagle woven into it.

Everyone hugged and kissed Alan, and pride shone in the Wizard's eyes.

Alan rested his hand on Joyhopper's head, and then he looked up into the sky where Eagle soared in lazy circles above them. Alan turned and met the Wizard's gaze. The old man winked.

Alan nodded. He knew he would meet Eagle again one day.

Gold on the Mountain

Tell us, tell us!" the animals begged. "Please, Joyhopper. Please?" They pushed him toward the center of the Small Golden Ring.

Mouse yanked at Joyhopper's ear. "Hurry up!"

Badger shoved at Joyhopper's feet. "Get in there!"

By the time they had finished pushing, pulling, and dragging Joyhopper across the grass into the Ring, they were all laughing so hard they could only lie in a tangle of fur and whiskers, legs and tails.

"All right, all right!" Joyhopper gasped through his giggles. "I'll tell you what it was like when I went with Eagle."

The other animals fell silent. They sat up, their ears pricked forward, eager to hear his story.

"Well," said Joyhopper, his nose wiggling as he breathed in the clear, crisp air, "the Wizard had asked me if I would help with a test for Alan Unstuck. At first, I said, 'Of course,' but when I heard what I'd have to do, I was scared. The thought of letting Eagle carry me away was frightening. But I knew the Wizard wouldn't have asked me if I weren't ready."

Bear and Ant nodded.

"What did it feel like?" squeaked Mouse. "Did it hurt?"

Joyhopper shook his head. "Eagle was very gentle. I barely felt her talons." He smiled at Ant. "When I was up there with her, high above the Glen, riding the Wind and seeing everything below me, I understood how you felt."

Ant sighed and nodded.

"Eagle set me down in a field high on the mountain," Joyhopper continued. "As I was hopping around there, an old woman came to me. She spoke to me kindly, and she gave me Good Food. Then she lifted me into her arms, beneath her cloak, and after awhile, I heard her speaking with Alan. Once Alan had passed his test and left, the Eagle Woman asked me what reward I would like for my courage. She told me I could make a wish."

"A wish!" breathed Ant. He imagined himself soaring in his own airplane.

"A wish!" murmured Owl, picturing himself with a PhD in High Language.

Tale Eleven: Gold on the Mountain

Fawn nudged the others, turning their attention back to Joyhopper. "What did you wish?" she asked him.

Before Joyhopper could answer, the Indigo Wizard came toward them, carrying a big box wrapped in gold paper. He set the box down on the ground within the circle of animals.

"What is it?" asked Turtle.

"It looks like a present to me," said the Wizard.

"Who's it from?" piped Mouse.

"Well, let's see." The Wizard reached into the folds of his cloak and pulled out a pair of wire-rimmed glasses. He perched them on his nose and leaned forward to peer at the tag on the box. "For Joyhopper," he read.

"Oh!" sighed Ant. "It's your reward, Joyhopper."

"What do you think it is?" whispered Fawn.

"Only one way to find out," said the Wizard.

Joyhopped hopped up to the box. He carefully unwrapped the gold paper, and then he slowly lifted the lid. Reaching a paw inside, he pulled out a solid gold eagle's feather. A piece of paper fluttered out as well, and the Wizard picked it up and read it:

"You hold within your hand reward
*   for courage great and true.*
The feather of your wish does come
*   from Eagle's breast to you.*
Hold it in your hand and heart,
*   let it kindle fire.*

Look upon the gold above
to see your heart's desire."

The animals gazed up at the high mountain. The sun shone golden on its peaks.

Joyhopper looked down at the feather clasped in his paw. He felt it tingle, as though the sunlight made it vibrate.

"You're so lucky!" Fawn said.

The Wizard nodded. "This is a marvelous reward, Joyhopper. Can you tell us how you knew to ask for this?"

Joyhopper looked at the Wizard. "I didn't."

"You didn't?" asked Bear. "What *did* you ask for?"

"I asked Eagle that all my friends in the Glen would have their dreams come true, forever and ever and ever."

The other animals looked at the Golden Feather, and they realized it was for all of them. They threw their arms around Joyhopper. "Let us call it the Eagle Feather of Hearts' Dreams," pronounced Owl.

"We'll put it where we can all see it whenever we want," said Joyhopper, and he carried it to the Ancient Oak beside the Crystal Pool. "There!" He stuck it in a niche in the tree's bark.

The animals looked at the feather. It shimmered in the light from the sun.

"Look!" said Fawn and pointed toward the mountain above their heads. "Gold on the Mountain."

The high mountain was bathed in light that shone as bright as the feather.

And from then on, the Glen family has gathered once a year so that each of the animals can hold the Eagle Feather of Hearts' Dreams and gaze at the Gold

on the Mountain. Wonderful things have happened in the Glen because of their wishes on that day.

But that is another story. . . .